Music Quotes
COLORING BOOK

BY JENNIFER BOSTER

"Music gives a **soul** to the universe, **wings** to the mind, **flight** to the imagination and **life** to everything."

— Plato

Music is the universal Language of Mankind.

— Henry Wadsworth Longfellow

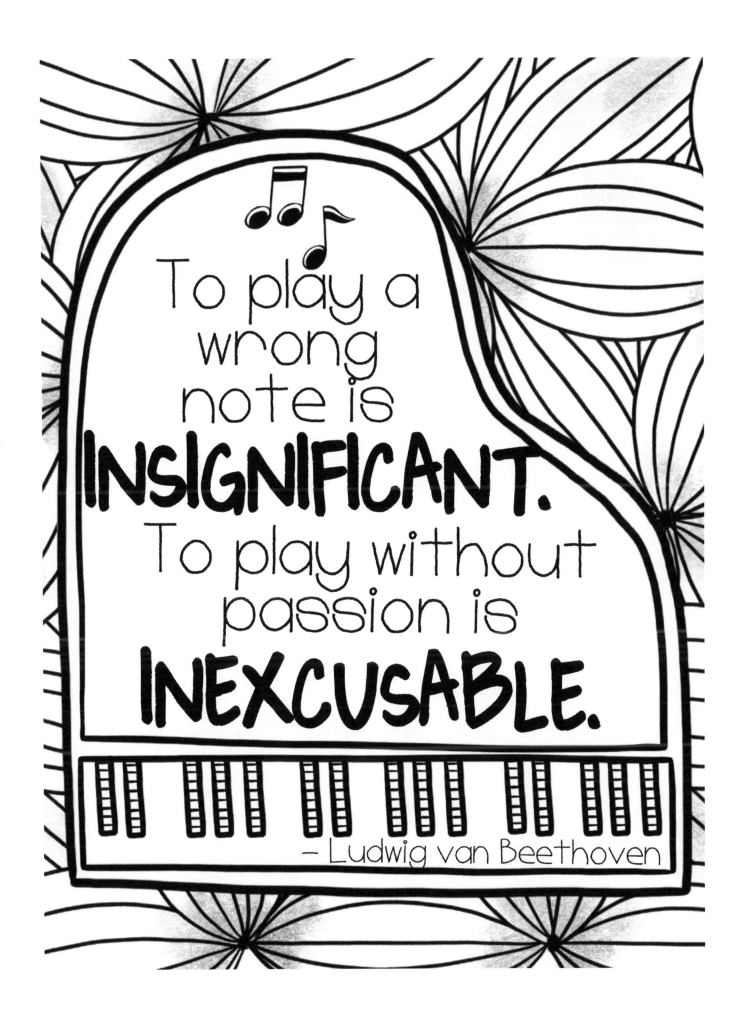

Life

SEEMS TO GO ON

WITHOUT EFFORT

WHEN I AM

FILLED WITH

Music

- GEORGE ELIOT

There is music in
every child.

The teacher's job
is to find it &
nurture it.
- Frances Clark

MUSIC IS ENOUGH FOR A LIFETIME, BUT A LIFETIME IS NOT ENOUGH FOR MUSIC.

- SERGEI RACHMANINOFF

A great song should lift your heart, warm the soul and make you feel good.
—Colbie Caillat

Music & Art are the guiding Lights of the world.

- Pablo Picasso

A MAN SHOULD HEAR A
LITTLE *music*, READ A
LITTLE *poetry* AND SEE A
FINE *picture* EVERY DAY
OF HIS LIFE, IN ORDER THAT
WORLDLY CARES MAY NOT
OBLITERATE THE SENSE OF
THE *beautiful* WHICH
GOD HAS IMPLANTED IN THE
HUMAN SOUL.

-GOETHE

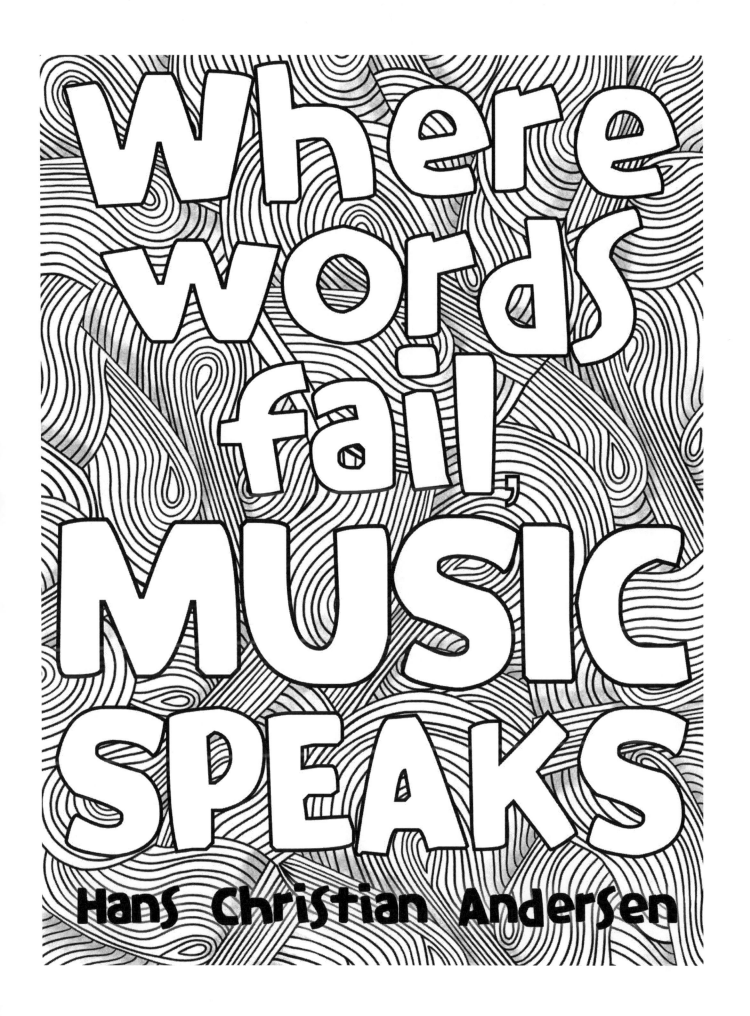

Life is like
a piano -
it needs the

Master's
touch

- Unknown

Music
washes away from the soul the Dust of everyday Life.
– Berthold Auerbach

For the first time, he heard something that he knew to be music.

He heard people singing.

Behind him, across vast distances of space and time, from the place he had left,

he thought he heard music too. But perhaps, it was only an echo.

- Lois Lowry

The *aim* and final end of all *music* should be none other than the *glory of God* and the refreshment of the *soul.*

- J.S. Bach

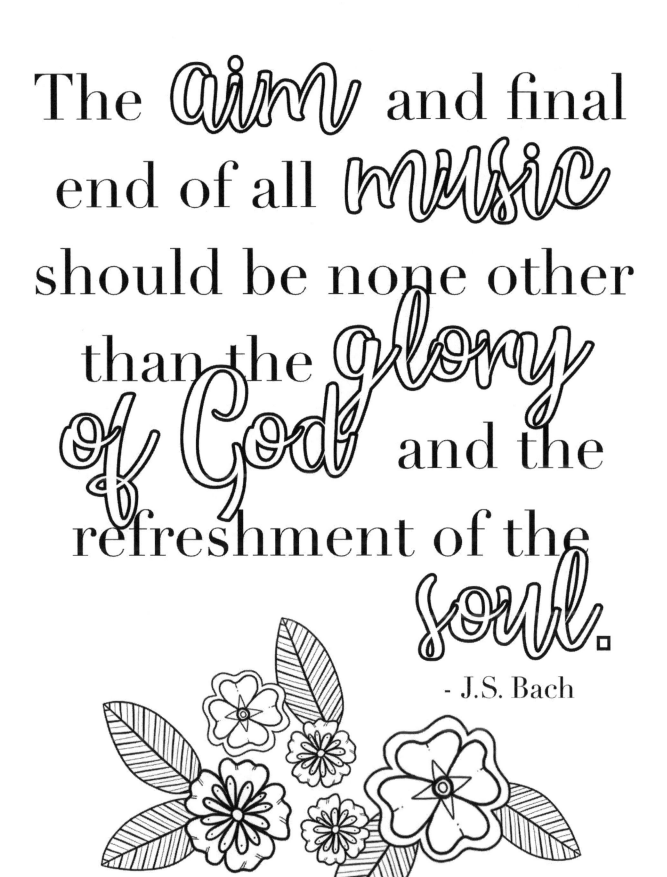

Did you enjoy this book? Please help me get the word out by leaving me an Amazon review!

More music-themed coloring books from Jennifer Boster:

Shades of Sound: Women Composers
Shades of Sound: Spring
Shades of Sound: Christmas
Shades of Sound: America
and many more!

Visit theplayfulpiano.com to learn more!

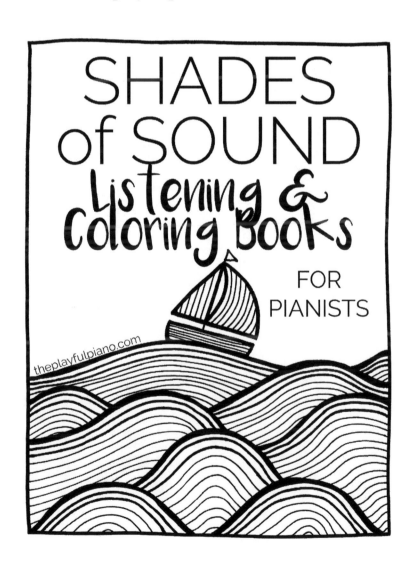

About the Author

Jenny Boster has been playing the piano and drawing ever since she was a little girl. She loves combining her interests to create fun and original resources for piano teachers. She has loved teaching piano lessons for twenty years! Jenny has a Bachelor of Music degree in Piano Performance from Brigham Young University and is a Nationally-Certified Teacher of Music. Jenny is passionate about encouraging students to listen to and gain a love for classical music. Her greatest joys are her husband, Jonathan, and being a mother to her five children.